The Breakup Book

To the boy who broke my heart,
to my mom who tried to warn me,
to Jiminy Cricket for keeping me
company along the way, and most
importantly, to my girlfriends who
always brought the map and who
were crazy enough to come along
for the ride.

The Breakup Book

...A Girl's Guide to Putting the Pieces Back Together

by Diane Mastromarino

Blue Mountain Press™

SPS Studios, Inc., Boulder, Colorado

Library of Congress Catalog Card Number: 2002006624
ISBN: 0-88396-668-9

ACKNOWLEDGMENTS appear on page 64.

Certain trademarks are used under license.

Manufactured in the United States of America.
Second Printing: 2003

 This book is printed on recycled paper.

This book is printed on fine quality, laid embossed, 80 lb. paper. This paper has been specially produced to be acid free (neutral pH) and contains no groundwood or unbleached pulp. It conforms with the requirements of the American National Standards Institute, Inc., so as to ensure that this book will last and be enjoyed by future generations.

Library of Congress Cataloging-in-Publication Data

Mastromarino, Diane, 1978-
    The breakup book : a girl's guide to putting the pieces back together
/ by Diane Mastomarino.
        p. cm.
    ISBN 0-88396-668-9 (alk. paper)
    1. Man-woman relationships. 2. Separation (Psychology). 3. Single
women—Psychology. I. Title.
    HQ801 .M425 2002
    306.7—dc21

                                                                2002006624
                                                                      CIP

SPS Studios, Inc.

P.O. Box 4549, Boulder, Colorado 80306

Contents

Begin with This...

There always comes a time of elimination. The earth
sheds each year. The trees and flowers let go of their
identity. As the old identity dies, a new identity is
born. The body sheds constantly. Some of it happens
invisibly, so naturally and silently that we do not
realize it is happening. The heart and the spirit also
shed. They shed the emotions and experiences that
we no longer need. They shed the things that stunt our
growth. This, too, is an invisible process. Yet because of
the energy involved, the emotional energy, we often
feel the emotional and spiritual shedding. It feels as if
we are dying. We are. Just like the flowers and the
trees, we are dying to an old identity. This shedding,
or death, is not the end of us. It is the beginning.

— Iyanla Vanzant

Suddenly Single

You can see it in his eyes. You can tell in his mannerisms, the way he touches his face uncomfortably with one hand and shifts his weight from right to left, left to right. If he chooses the easy way out, to hide his apprehension behind a telephone line, then you can hear it in the way his voice quivers a little bit when saying hello. And then there is that brief silence as he struggles to find the words he rehearsed over and over again the night before. The words that in this moment hold the strength to break a heart into a thousand pieces, the power to bring a grown woman to sob like a child who has just skinned her knee. And as he walks away or slowly places the telephone onto its cradle, you stand dumbfounded, choking on the lump that has formed in your throat midway between "It's not you, it's me..." and "I'd really like to still be friends..."

In one moment, you go from being a happy couple to being two separate beings again — except you can't remember what it means to be separate, to be alone. In fact, you can't remember much about life before he charmed his way into your heart, promising that he was different. But you were whole before his arrival and will continue to be so after his departure. So fasten your seat belt, because this ride just may be a bit bumpy. The destination, however, is well worth the wait.

Just think of it... **single**. You ponder the word over and over in your head. At first it brings tears. **Single**. Say it with me. You are suddenly single and it's the suddenly part that is hurting so much — kind of like a rug pulled quickly from under your feet. This change was so unexpected, unwelcomed even, but now that it has happened, you must pick yourself up off the floor, dust yourself off, and realize that the single part really isn't so bad. In fact, it has a million advantages waiting to be discovered. So say it with me... **SINGLE** — scream it out loud. And know that this isn't an end. It's just the beginning.

First Minutes
of SiNGLe

First impulse: To hunt him down with the plan to *calmly* explain to him that he's made an enormous mistake by letting you go.

What will really happen: Calm for you at this point would be sobbing uncontrollably while reciting love poetry and recalling the one hundred best moments the two of you had together (as if he didn't experience them firsthand). And then before leaving, you deposit every picture, every dried flower, and every article of clothing including his socks into his open arms hoping he'll drop them and hold you close to him, begging you to stay. However, because the tears falling from your eyes and the runny nose you casually wipe on your sleeve are NOT a turn-on... and because as you are professing your love to him, he is thinking about putting on the basketball shorts you just handed him and going to shoot some hoops with the guys... this does not happen.

A bit of advice: Steer clear of your ex. Just in case you are unsure of what that entails, please refrain from the following: calling to say hello, calling to say you love him, calling to hear his voice and then to hang up immediately following his "hello," writing a meaningful e-mail, writing a mean e-mail, driving by his house to see how he is doing, driving by his work to see if his car is there, driving past his best friend's house to see if he has told him yet, packing up his belongings and leaving them on his doorstep, doing anything at all that would give him any knowledge that you still care and that your life has been disrupted in any way.

Second impulse: Call his best friend, who has also become a good friend of yours while the two of you were dating, and ask him to call your ex (yes, he is your ex now) and talk to him for you.

What will really happen: Though this may sound like an excellent idea because this friend has always held you in high regard, he still remains the best friend of your ex. So regardless of how many times he has told you he loves the two of you together and thinks you're a wonderful person, he is still classified as the opposition. If you call and say, "Please don't tell him I called you," or "I'm doing okay," in between sobs, chances are he will recite your conversation five minutes later to your ex, blowing his nose comically on his sleeve to get the details just right. They will then discuss tonight's game or tomorrow's tee time. This also goes for his mother, sister, great-aunt, or any other family member of his.

A bit of advice: No matter how much it seemed that you had become part of his circle, the fact remains that as of this moment, the two of you are no longer together. His family members may be saddened that they won't be seeing you at the next family picnic and his friends may miss chatting with you at the next party, but their lives will go on, as will yours. So, do yourself a favor, and don't get them involved. They will probably put in their two cents anyway, and it would look a lot better if you didn't have to force them to do so.

Third impulse: Hang yourself by the cord of your curling iron or overdose on some chewable vitamins.

What will really happen: The thought seems somewhat sane at this moment. You would leave a lengthy letter, doused in your sweetest perfume, telling him you couldn't live without him. You would wear the dress he deemed his favorite and he would sob uncontrollably, begging you to come back to him. This seemingly romantic plan that looks so enticing in the movies is not very practical at all. Though your ex may be overwhelmed with grief, not to mention guilt, you will no longer be around to experience it. Where is the real satisfaction in that? And to top it all off, that guilt will subside and his life will continue on: he getting off easy, you six feet under.

A bit of advice: This master plan to get back at him for hurting you will undoubtedly be a huge flop, besides leaving behind many innocent bystanders (such as your family and friends) to grieve for your sudden departure. So if these thoughts do find their way into your head, shake them out immediately. Turn to those around you for help. Once you make it through these first difficult moments, the rest will somehow fall into place. Just give it time.

Fourth impulse: Seek revenge. Why?... Because your heart is hurting, because he promised he was different, because you had already picked out bridesmaids' dresses and practiced signing your name with his (no hyphen) on every single notebook you own.

What will really happen: Though the saying goes that revenge is sweet, it is way too soon to begin plotting yours. In these very fiery beginning stages, you are borderline combustible. Revenge at this point would probably consist of blowing up his house, pulling out his toenails one by one with a pair of pliers, or following in the footsteps of your newfound role model, Lorena Bobbitt. Though all of these sound extremely rewarding at this moment in time, none of them will pan out as planned in the end. With your luck, you will wind up with ten years and he will not even come to visit you.

A bit of advice: Pencil revenge in on your calendar for a later date, when you are feeling a bit more rational and your plan doesn't include power tools or kitchenware. When that time comes around, you will be able to distinguish between sanity and lunacy, and you'll find a quiet, hit-him-below-the-belt type of revenge instead of the front-page-Sunday-morning-psychopathic-killer kind. You don't need to make the headlines to get him where it really hurts. You just need to give yourself time to let this all seep in. Once you have let some pass, chances are that revenge will become much less of a priority. It will probably move close to the bottom of your list following taking out the trash and cleaning your bathtub.

The Breakup Process

(sad but true)

Boy breaks up with Girl...

Girl cries
and makes a scene...

Boy acts like he feels
horrible, but is secretly filled
with satisfaction from
knowing that he IS that
important...

YOUR JOB:
Stop the Madness

STOP

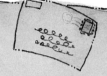

Surprise Him

An ex expects tears. He expects his phone to be ringing off the wall and his in box to be swamped with messages. He even expects the melodramatic return of his things and an "I'm-okay-no-thanks-to-you" letter a few weeks down the line. A scorned lover can be ever so predictable.

You want to undermine the breakup process and try as hard as possible not to play the role he expects you to play. The key to not being "that girl" is simply to be busy... be very busy. Be so busy that your thoughts are clouded by the things you are doing now, and even more so, by the things you will do tomorrow. Make plans, make lunch dates, and take coffee breaks. Make to-do lists and shopping lists. Buy a new address book: the ultimate purchase for starting over. This will take you hours to update, and why not dial a few of those numbers to chat about how well you are doing (not his number, of course)? Buy a new daily planner, and plan to be busy. Be busy doing anything that will keep you from being busy concentrating on your ex, because that kind of busy will result in disaster.

Don't Be "that girl"

We already have enough men so high on their horses they need a ladder to get down; your ex does not need to join this army. And you, single-handedly, have the power to keep this from happening. All it takes is a little willpower and a lot of self-control. (Oh, and a huge container of your very favorite ice cream is always helpful.)

Fight back those urges that will only prove to your ex that he is a necessity in your life:

1) Don't drown him in love... he will swim away.

2) Don't beg him to stay... he might.

3) Don't worship the ground he walks on... he will walk right off into someone else's arms.

Don't drown him in love... he will swim away.

By smothering him with letters and phone calls to try to convince him how good you were together, you are essentially pushing him further and further away. As you drive by his house twenty-four times a day, stopping three of those times to tell him... first; how much you love him, second; how much you miss him, and third; that you are doing just fine without him, he is plotting in his head which city he can move to the fastest.

Give him a little credit. He knows how good you were together. He played the part of your boyfriend, if you remember correctly, and can replay all your wonderful memories and moments in his head at any time he pleases. He doesn't need you to remind him. Paying him too much attention will scare him further away, and it will not give him the chance to think about you in the way he should be.

Your absence is what will tug at his heartstrings, not your voice whimpering sweet nothings into the telephone line. If you give him five minutes to miss you, he may begin to feel the emptiness that has formed in his life since you've been gone. Let him wonder what you are doing, who you are with, and how you are feeling. He was your boyfriend and you were his girlfriend, and so regardless of this sudden decision to make your relationship otherwise, he did, and probably still does care about you; the key is to give him the chance to realize it.

Don't beg him to stay... he might.

Many girls make the mistake of thinking that if they try hard enough, they can stop a relationship from ending. They attempt to win their lover back by convincing him that things will be better. They say that they will change the kind of person they are or the way they live their life when really they are perfect just the way they are. In order to win this battle, some girls will do just about anything to keep their relationship alive, but these attempts to get him to stay will ultimately fail, whether it is now or a few weeks down the road.

It is possible that your ex may decide to stick around for a little while longer... a few weeks, a month even. But you will walk on eggshells for most of your time together, and he will have his cake and probably have the fortune of eating it too. You will not be yourself out of fear that he will leave again, and depending on the type of guy he is, he can definitely use this knowledge against you. And one day, down the road, the reasons he left in the first place will surface yet again, and sadly, the grand finale will be the same.

It is better to let him go than to beg him to stay, because if you succeed he may be staying for the wrong reasons, and that will end badly for both of you. If he goes, yes, you will be sad, but you may realize that you are better off without him. Or you and he may both realize that you are better off together. Letting him go is the only way to know this for sure.

Don't worship the ground he walks on... he may walk right off into someone else's arms.

By professing your love to him and practically begging him to take you back... by letting him see that he has the power to disrupt one woman's sleeping, eating, and all-around living patterns in just one moment... by telling him how truly wonderful you think he is despite the heartbreak you are experiencing... you are basically asking him to find a new girlfriend — or many girlfriends, for that matter. This amount of attention would make anyone a bit overconfident. And it is that newfound feeling of importance that will send him off in search of other girls he now feels are in need of being graced with his presence.

The last thing you want is for him to feel self-assured and overconfident, walking around town thinking he is God's gift to the female population. The male ego is so easily inflated and so in this situation, it is your job to burst his bubble. Act like you are okay, even if you are not... hold in the tears for one last second until he is out of sight... be strong, and remember that any crazed attempts to get him back may not only push him further away, but possibly into someone else's arms. So the moral of the story is — don't be so impulsive.

What to Do

Rethink the impulses. If you have to lock yourself in your room and chain yourself to your bed, do it!

Disconnect the phone and **don't** resort to e-mail (it *is* just as bad).

Look in the mirror and tell yourself you don't want him to see you this way: bloodshot eyes, runny nose. It is just not attractive.

Remind yourself that this is for now. This is nothing but a minor setback in the great scheme of things and you will be okay. You will be more than okay.

Run a hot shower or bath and soak. Soak away all your stresses and all your heartache. Clear your mind of all your thoughts, both good and bad, and truly relax.

Look in the mirror and tell yourself how beautiful you are, how strong you were before this, and how much stronger this will make you. And most importantly, remind yourself how unlucky he is. You haven't lost; he lost you.

Make a pact with yourself that you will get through this... maybe not today or tomorrow morning, but soon... soon you will start over better than before.

This is reality sinking in —
This is the tingling in your limbs and the knot
    in your stomach coming full term
This is the scene of the movie that calls for
    (a lot of) tissues
This is the part nobody said would be easy —
    the hardest part of all parts
And once these moments pass —
Once you release the tension that has
    settled in your temples
And the butterflies that linger
    set off for the horizon
The strength will rise from somewhere within
    and you will finally be free

It's Okay to Be Sad

It really is okay to be sad. There's no reason to wear a goofy smiley face to convince the world that you are just fine. * You need to give this a chance to sink in and to become real for you. That may take a day or a weekend or even a week. Right now, the only person that matters is you. If you keep what you're feeling bottled up inside, you will not be able to start your healing process. So let it out, and don't be afraid to feel.

Pull your knees into your chest and wrap your arms around them tightly to keep you from falling apart. Then slowly let them go. You will find that with your feet spread out in front of you, with your limbs free and flowing, you are still whole.

This is part of the acceptance, the realization that this relationship has come to an end — and miraculously, you are still alive.

* This goofy smiley face, however, is not optional if by chance you run into your ex. Then a smiley face becomes essential in order to reinforce the fact that you are fine without him.

For the hurt you feel right now at this moment...

*For all the times you've wanted to, but choked back
the tears...*

*For the times in the future when things will go wrong,
but out of embarrassment or pride
you will hold back...*

Cry a little. Cry a lot.

Yesterday, I Cried

Yesterday, I cried.

I came home, went straight to my room, sat on the edge of my bed,
  kicked off my shoes, unhooked my bra,
  and had myself a good cry.

I'm telling you,

  I cried until my nose was running all over the silk blouse I
    got on sale.

  I cried until my ears were hot.

  I cried until my head was hurting so bad
    that I could hardly see the pile of soiled tissues
    lying on the floor at my feet.

I want you to understand,

  I had myself a really good cry yesterday.

Yesterday, I cried,

  for all the days that I was too busy, or too tired,
    or too mad to cry.

I cried for all the days, and all the ways,

  and all the times I had dishonored, disrespected,
    and disconnected my Self from myself,

  only to have it reflected back to me in the ways
    others did to me

  the same things I had already done to myself.

I cried for all the things I had given, only to have them stolen;
   for all the things I asked for that had yet to show up;
   for all the things I had accomplished, only to give
      them away, to people in circumstances,
   which left me feeling empty, and battered and
      plain old used.
I cried because there really does come a time when the
   only thing left for you to do is cry....
Yesterday, I cried.
I cried because I hurt. I cried because I was hurt.
I cried because hurt has no place to go
   except deeper into the pain that caused it in the first place,
   and when it gets there, the hurt wakes you up.
I cried because it was too late. I cried because it was time.
I cried because my soul knew that I didn't know
   that my soul knew everything I needed to know.
I cried a soulful cry yesterday, and it felt so good.
It felt so very, very bad.
In the midst of my crying, I felt my freedom coming,
Because
Yesterday, I cried
   with an agenda.

— Iyanla Vanzant

Here's the Plan

It's time to get your life back in order. Don't try to take things too fast — the truth is that it's not going to happen overnight. When you wake up tomorrow, your heart is still going to hurt. But the good news is that every day, it's going to hurt a little bit less. As long as you keep moving forward and keep looking toward tomorrow, you're going to make it through this.

Don't give in to those feelings of helplessness. There are things you can do to help yourself get through this time. Instead of focusing all your thoughts on him, remind yourself of all the people in your life who care about you. Let them comfort you. But even more importantly, learn to comfort yourself. Don't let yourself believe that you're nothing without him. Think back to all the happy times you had before you ever met him. Those memories are proof that you can be happy on your own.

You're going to get through this. Just keep telling yourself that until you start to believe it.

— Natalie Evans

How Long Will It Take?

The After Math: Breakup Algebra

$$D = R\left(\frac{1}{b} + \frac{p+f}{l} + \pi s^3\right) \times T(v + c + a)$$

D = *HOW LONG IT WILL TAKE TO DISTANCE YOURSELF (in months)*

R = *RATE his looks on a scale from 1 to 10*

T = *amount of TIME you were together (months)*

b = *number of times you've already BROKEN UP*

p = *0 if your PARENTS liked him*
p = *5 if your PARENTS didn't like him*

f = *number of close FRIENDS you have in common,* except
f = *1,439 if you have no other FRIENDS*

l = *number of miles away he LIVES,* except
l = *0.5 if you LIVED together*

s = *volume of his STUFF that you're secretly keeping*

v = *tan (number of tropical VACATIONS you've taken together)*
c = *sin (number of times he CHEATED on you)*
    {use 1/c if you cheated on him}
a = *cosine (amount of money you have in joint checking ACCOUNT)*

— *Lynn Harris*

Two Bowls of Ice Cream, One Spoon

Regardless of the public's opinion that following a breakup we should instantaneously bounce back, get over it, go out in the world, and move on, we all need our sob time, our container-of-ice-cream time and our curl-into-bed-and-feel-sorry-for-ourselves time. You are in a difficult place right now, and you can't brush your feelings under the carpet and hope they will go away. It will take a little bit of time away from the world to be able to dive back into it. This is not to say that you should survive one year on thirty gallons of chocolate fudge swirl, 365 tragic love stories, and a wardrobe consisting of *his* old worn T-shirt, a pair of flannel pants, and some fuzzy slippers. A few days, even a week of sulking time is definitely allowed to bandage up your heart, but this is just a rest period, a time to figure out how to tackle this head-on so you can get on with the rest of your life.

Accept... that loneliness has healing qualities. A period of time alone with oneself allows introspection, reflection, growth and development of the inner self. Hollowness and emptiness are replaced by inner fullness and strength. You have made a giant step toward independence when you are comfortable by yourself, no longer dependent on the company of others.

— *Bruce Fisher*

Take a personal day off from work or school and sleep in. Take a very long bath or shower and use up all the hot water. This is a selfish, take-care-of-you time in your life. Fill up not one, but two bowls with your favorite ice cream, relax on the couch and indulge. Rent a classic love story or read your favorite book. If you feel sadness, cry. If you feel anger, jump on your bed and throw a childish temper tantrum. This is your alone time to release all your negative energy and come to terms with the changes in your life. Do whatever you need to do at this moment to make your heart feel better, but remember that this is extremely temporary — you can even categorize it as a fleeting moment. Soon you will need to pick yourself up off the couch, throw out that ratty old T-shirt, and realize that the world doesn't stop because you are hurting. It will continue to go on whether you choose to join it or not, so you may as well jump on for the ride.

Even though unwanted loss comes into everyone's life, each of us chooses how to respond to that loss. After we have ached with anguish, cried until no more tears will come, and hated the world and everything in it, there comes a point in our lives when we must choose how we're going to respond to what life has handed us.

— *Barbara Hansen, Ph.D.*

Things to Do with...
Photos of Your Evil Ex

Dartboard bull's-eye.

Write embarrassing... stats on back,
laminate, and trade with all your friends.

Pop a bunch into the Cuisinart
and turn into confetti for your
next New Year's party.

Mail off to inmates in local prisons with a
touching and titillating letter of introduction.
(Include your ex's return address
and phone number, of course.)

Use packing tape to adhere
to soccer balls, baseball bats,
or bowling balls.

Spread one inch apart on
ungreased cookie sheet
and broil on high.

Stick to grille of car to catch
high-speed bug splats.

Bury in backyard with a dead fish.

Build a desperate loser's website
to help him meet new chicks.

Drain toilet and superglue photo
to bottom of toilet bowl.

Line the bottom of your birdcage
or cat litter box.

— Cameron Tuttle

Shoulder Padding

It is time to take all those close friends who have claimed that they would always be there for you up on their offer. You need some shoulders to cry on and some friendly faces who can rip your ex to shreds, picking and choosing all the annoying quirks and faults that kept him from achieving the Mr. America title while you were together. You need someone to tell you how wonderful you are, how much better you can do, and how they never liked him anyway. All these things will provide padding for your fall.

If you find yourself repeating over and over that you're fine, that this is no big deal, and that you'd rather be alone, chances are you're lying to others, as well as to yourself. These feelings you are suppressing will at some point bubble to the surface and explode like a giant volcano, probably over something as small as a set of misplaced car keys or an empty container of milk.

The first moments of a breakup are filled with a feeling of emptiness, but as the people who care about you most offer their understanding and support, you should realize that you are less alone than you have ever been. It will feel like a huge weight is lifted as you talk to the people you trust. Lean on them, and use the strength they offer to heal your wounds and rediscover your own strength.

Give sorrow words; the grief that does not speak whispers the o'er fraught heart and bids it to break.

— *William Shakespeare*

It's Okay

It's okay to be afraid
of the things we don't understand.
It's okay to feel anxious
when things aren't working our way.
It's okay to feel lonely...
even when you're with other people.
It's okay to feel unfulfilled
because you know something is missing
(even if you're not sure what it is).
It's okay to think and worry and cry.

It's okay to do
whatever you have to do, but
just remember, too,
that eventually you're going to
adjust to the changes life brings your way,
and you'll realize that
it's okay to love again and laugh again,
and it's okay to get to the point where
the life you live
is full and satisfying and good to you...
and it will be that way
because you made it that way.

— Laine Parsons

You're Luckier than You Think

Despite the pain you felt when he left and the amount of tissues you went through to wipe away the tears (not to mention the late charges on your library card from rereading a zillion and one love stories), you must remember one wonderful thing that came of all this... you have loved. When love comes along, there are no promises that it will stick around forever. There are no contracts that guarantee at least ten years or the exclusion of a broken heart. Falling in love is like falling backwards and hoping someone will catch you. Sometimes you get lucky and other times you're left on the floor with a bump on your head and a huge feeling of disappointment.

Some people in this world search endlessly for the kind of love you once had in your relationship. Some people never find another person to share any part of their life with at all. Yes, your breakup makes you sad, but think of the people who live their lives alone, never feeling the happiness you enjoyed, even if it was just for a short while. You should choke back the tears and relish your luck. You were fortunate enough to have loved at all.

Focus on those things that were good. Remember when it was a loving experience, and then let each other go without bitterness. Life is a journey you can't plan that teaches you to remember who you are. We choose our lives and all that happens, to learn and grow.

— *Suzanne Somers*

Whoever we are
we hold in our hearts
the memories
of the times
we have lived and loved.

Today is more meaningful
for it is built on
who we were,
where we have been
and the paths
we have traveled.

— *George Betts*

Rushing in for the Rebound

So you've technically been single for about an hour now and this kind of short, decent-looking, pretty-blue-eyed, available man has made his way across the coffeehouse to say hello to you. You push the hot chocolate with extra whipped cream you had planned to drown your sorrows in to the side and discreetly check his hand for a ring. You can barely hear him speaking about his occupation and where he went to high school over the wedding bells chiming in your head. You will not be alone, you think to yourself. You will show your ex how quickly you've bounced back. But the truth is, you are not as resilient as a rubber band, and by your third date you will probably find yourself rambling about your ex, the words flowing from your mouth like a waterfall.

Chances are if this new guy likes you he'll comfort you, and you will keep him around for the sake of not being alone. And somewhere down the road, this will end badly for both of you. Though it may seem easier to quickly find a replacement for your ex, rushing into a new relationship is not the answer. Sending yourself on a wild-goose chase for "Mr. Right" will most likely result in numerous "Mr. Wrongs." Get comfortable with being single before you seek out another relationship. Once you feel ready to date, start out slow. Date casually before you dive headfirst into another long-term relationship... for your sake and for the sake of the poor boy you will later need to refer to as your "rebound."

Date Yourself
with Style and Sensitivity

- Eat over the sink by candlelight.

- Treat yourself to a new sexy outfit.

- When you catch your reflection in a store window, flirt shamelessly.

- Buy yourself flowers every week.

- Plan fun weekend getaways to romantic spots.

- Turn the music up and the lights down and slow-dance barefoot in the kitchen.

- Gently caress your hand or thigh at the movies.

- Sleep in your slinkiest nightgown or nothing at all.

- Whisper sweet nothings into the air, then spin around really fast to catch them in your ear.

- Take long walks in the moonlight, hand in hand, making plans for the future.

— Cameron Tuttle

Fall in Love with You

After this breakup, you are most likely feeling a little down on yourself, picking apart every flaw and turning it into a massive catastrophe. You've found every reason possible to blame yourself for the breakup, but chances are it really was him, not you. And regardless of his reasoning, blaming yourself is not going to win him back or allow you to get on with your life.

This is a chance to figure out who you are without someone to call your other half. This is a chance to be completely on your own and embrace who you are as an individual. This is a chance to fall in love with you. That concept may sound silly, but you'd be surprised how many women look in the mirror and wish they were someone else. There is no such thing as perfection, and the truth is that the grass will always appear greener on the other side.

You have so much to offer the world. And just because one lousy male didn't realize what he had, it doesn't mean that you are not worthy of being loved. You owe it to yourself to put yourself on a pedestal, comfort your heart, and tend to your needs. This breakup is not a time to feel sorry for yourself. It is a time to get to know yourself, to embrace the things you love, and to change the things you dislike. You must fall in love with yourself first... and then leave the rest up to fate.

Get to Know Yourself

Take the time to be alone,
so you can know just how terrific
your own company can be.
Remember that being alone
doesn't always mean being lonely;
it can be a beautiful experience
of finding your creativity,
your heartfelt feelings,
and the calm and quiet peace
deep inside you.

— Jacqueline Schiff

One Will Pass the Door

Your first duty is to learn to live in the world,
    for to this you are born.
But, meantime, make for yourself a secret room in
    the inner house of consciousness, where you may
    rest from the strain of the world, and disentangle
    yourself from that which is unworthy of your soul.
Into this room let no unsympathetic person enter,
    for he would laugh at you in the temple of your
    better self.
Yet, in a long time, perhaps someone
    who understands will pass the door.
    And who shall say what your life
    may be from that hour!

— Max Ehrmann

*T*ruly embrace forgiveness. Let go of the guilt that the past holds and free yourself of the strings that tie you down.

And fly.

Love yourself and your beautiful spirit. Love yourself when you feel abandoned, when being alone seems too much to take. And with the knowledge that somewhere, someone sits looking up at the stars and hopes you are doing well, smile to yourself. You are loved.

Open your mind to the unknown. Let your spirit dance among those who once seemed unusual. Absorb their wisdom, cast away your indifference, and offer a piece of yourself in return.

Never lose faith. Carry it with you like a coin in your pocket.

Choose laughter. Do it often and loudly, even in solitude... especially in solitude. Find the courage to laugh when it would be easier to cry. And do not just live, but be truly alive.

Chase dreams, the remarkable ones that once danced in your head as a child. Do not reach for other people's wishes, but find the stars you always longed to hold in the palm of your hand, and whisper to them that you are coming, that they will soon be yours.

Learn to trust, not only others, but yourself. Do not live in doubt, with constant questions circling in your head. Be certain. Be positive... even if you feel insecure. And do not blush if you have erred, because it is in our faults that we breed wisdom.

And there will be times when the course of life runs less than smooth. It is not all sunshine and rainbows. But it is from the darkness that we learn the beauty of light.

Dos...

Do brighten your apartment with a bouquet of beautiful flowers, many bouquets if you'd like. You deserve them.

Do shop. A new pair of shoes to match your new sexy dress is the perfect medicine.

Do have yourself a good cry when your heart is feeling sad and life is overwhelming.

Do have a cocktail to unwind. (If you happen to be under the legal drinking age feel free to substitute a Shirley Temple.)

Do put on your most comfy pajamas and curl up with an old book.

Do take long walks to clear your mind. Follow your heart wherever it takes you: through the park, to a friend's house, or better yet, to the nearest ice-cream parlor.

Do call your family and friends who will listen to you vent and then poke fun at your ex until your tears turn into laughter.

Do eat ice cream for dinner and save last week's leftovers for dessert. (Side note: there's no need to save room for dessert.)

Do go out for a night on the town and flirt with cute boys.

...and Don'ts

Don't leave the dried flowers he gave you for your birthday last year burning on his front porch.

Don't limit your shopping to what he did or didn't like. Buy something that you love and he would've hated.

Don't hold your feelings inside. Eventually they will bubble to the surface and explode like a huge volcanic eruption.

Don't drink too much and dial his number. The consequences inevitably will be bad.

Don't put on his old T-shirt and sweatpants and read old letters he wrote you.

Don't take walks past his house to see if he is home. He does have windows and will notice you... even with your baseball cap disguise.

Don't call his family and friends to vent about what has happened or to ask them to talk some sense into your ex.

Don't eat ice cream for breakfast, lunch, and dinner for the next four weeks and forget the address of your gym.

Don't go out for the night on the town to the place you know your ex will be and try to get him back.

Get Fit...

This section appropriately appears after you have eaten two bowls of ice cream with one spoon and spent a few days on the couch with your only means of exercise varying between lifting a spoon to your mouth and changing channels on your remote control. The time has come to stop feeling sorry for yourself and get your lazy body in gear. Looking good on the outside will make you feel ten times better on the inside. And if that's not motivation enough, looking good on the outside will make your ex, among other men, take a second look, stare a little, even drool a bit, and that kind of response will definitely make you feel good on the inside.

Today is the day. Get yourself out of bed and take a deep breath. Stretch your arms out and give yourself a huge hug, because today marks the beginning of a brand new, happier you.

If your finances allow, join a local gym. Have a trainer show you around so you will feel more comfortable with the facilities. Together, set up a routine that works for you, and make a pact with yourself to follow it. If necessary, set up a goal-and-reward system. For example: if you go to the gym four times a week for three weeks, treat yourself to a new pair of shoes or a massage. Ask a friend to join with you. Having someone to go along with makes the task of working out a lot less grueling, not to mention that gossiping while on the treadmill makes the activity a bit less mouse-like and a little more enjoyable. You can also join an individual class such as dance, kick-boxing, yoga, or aerobics. With a good, motivating instructor, these types of classes can be both enjoyable and beneficial.

If money is tight, lace up your sneakers and go for a brisk jog or walk. On your first day out, don't ask a friend to come along. Find a pace and a route that are comfortable for you. Take in the fresh air, but learn to pace your breathing. Don't overdo it. This isn't a race. Don't try to rush through this, but rather enjoy it. Bring a walkman and listen to music that is motivating for you; let it carry you away. At home, create a workout routine that fits into your schedule. You can do a set of sit-ups or push-ups in the short time it takes for the shower to heat up in the morning. You may also want to visit a local video store and purchase or rent an exercise, yoga, or muscle shaping video. Try not to vary your days or times, but rather work out each day at the same time, so your body gets into a specific routine. At first you may feel like you are dragging yourself to workout, but it will eventually become as habitual as brushing your teeth or eating breakfast.

The first time you look in the mirror and see a difference, it will not only be in your tummy or thighs, it will be in the overall you. You will no longer feel sorry for yourself because you will look and feel great. You are slowly picking up the pieces, one by one, and moving closer and closer to the "on-my-own-and-loving-it" you. Let's keep moving down that road.

...and Flaunt It

So you've been working out and eating right. That face that stares back at you in the mirror each morning no longer cringes at your bloodshot eyes and chubby thighs, but rather smiles at this amazing, strong, free-spirited woman standing before it. No need to feel vain, though. Just let that smile peek through and nod approvingly, because "Girl... you look fine."

When you were younger you loved to play "dress-up": throwing on extravagant gowns, too-high heels, and applying way too much blue eye shadow and pink lipstick. These days, you throw on any old thing to run to the grocery store or go see a movie. It's about time to regress a bit and find the little girl in you who once made gaudy a fashion statement.

Why, you ask? Because you just never know who you may run into at any point in the day, at any given location. These days, there's no such thing as "all dressed up and nowhere to go." Whether you're going to grab a cup of coffee or heading out for a night on the town, you should take pride in yourself and the way you look. It is when you least expect it that your soul mate (not yet discovered) will clumsily bump into you at the local market, causing the bundle of apples in your arms to fall to the ground. But (there is always a "but"), because you look outrageous in that cute skirt and little yellow T-shirt, he will offer to stick around and help you pick everything back up. You will then make small talk, keeping your cool, and as you leave, he will watch you walk into the distance, plotting when and where he will get to see you again.

Though you may not run into Romeo or Prince Charming, there is always that chance of running smack into your ex when you least expect it. And when that happens, you will keep your cool because you looked in the mirror this morning and are well aware of how good you look. You will not get flustered and turn that awful shade of pink that will clash with your lavender turtleneck. You will not sit and make small talk because he is not worthy of your time. You will casually say hi and if he asks, you will say you are doing good, really good, but will not disclose any other information about your current life. (This does include the small white lie about moving to Venice with your new lover. That would be way too obvious.) He will notice how astounding you look, and this alone is proof enough that this breakup has really agreed with you. You can then go home and look at old pictures of the two of you together while inhaling one bowl (not two) of low-fat frozen yogurt to appease the knot that has returned to your throat and the butterflies that have found their way back into your stomach. There are still some pieces of your heart lingering around since he left and we mustn't overlook the fact that certain circumstances can reawaken the pain.

So for these reasons, and just simply because when you look better, you tend to feel better, always leave the house looking your best. This isn't to say you must go grocery shopping in a ball gown, but do change the white shirt with the grease stain on the sleeve, brush your hair, and reapply some lipstick... because you just never know.

Quick Fix-Its

Pamper Yourself

- Get a massage.

- Dye your hair a color he would hate.

- Read a book in the sun.

- Get a manicure.

- Spend a day in your pajamas.

- Buy a new perfume.

- Sleep in.

- Plan a road trip.

- Soak in a warm bath.

- Go to the zoo.

- Buy a bouquet of sunflowers.

- Do anything that makes you happy.

Do All the Things He Always Hated

- Stop and ask several strangers for directions.

- Change your order at least four times before deciding on what to eat.

- Don't shave your legs for a week.

- Wear a low-cut blouse and a tight pencil skirt and go to a place where you know you will see his friends — and flirt.

- Stay on the phone with a girlfriend for an hour.

- Eat beef jerky.

- Listen to show tunes and sing along at the top of your lungs.

— Suzanne Yalof

Dwell on His Flaws*

(*this one is worthy of two pages, for there are many)

- Not being able to keep a secret.

- Calling you by embarrassing pet names in public.

- Treating his remote control like his best friend.

- Acting like a two-year-old when he's sick.

- Chewing with his mouth open.

- Leaving his stinky clothes all over the house.

- Thinking that eating at McDonald's is going out to dinner.

- Singing the wrong words to songs on the radio.

- Commenting on how good looking other girls are.

- Walking on a clean floor or rug with muddy shoes.

- Not calling when he says he will.

- Believing that expressing feelings is only for girls.

- Thinking that eating hot dogs at a baseball game constitutes a romantic meal.

- *Transforming into a different man in front of his friends.*

- *Complaining endlessly about attending family functions.*

- *Talking about his ex-girlfriend.*

- *Pretending to listen but really having no idea what you are saying.*

- *Thinking that grunting is actually a healthy conversation.*

- *Watching "Sports Center" over and over as if the replay game will end differently.*

- *Driving a hundred miles an hour only to come to a sudden halt at the next red light.*

- *Comparing every meal you cook to his mother's.*

- *Thinking that belching the alphabet is a cool thing to do.*

- *Licking the bowl and considering it clean.*

- *Calling you at 4 a.m. after drinking way too much.*

- *Saying that he is different from other guys when really he's just the same.*

Write a Letter... and Throw It Away

It's been a while since the breakup, and by now you may have even forgotten the exact phrase your ex used and how much the initial shock hurt. You have slowly been picking up the pieces one by one. You almost feel whole some days; life has moved on and you have moved further and further away from feeling broken. There are other days, however, when it seems like the walls are caving in. Everything reminds you of him: the smell of a passerby's cologne, the song on the radio, an old shirt of his tucked in the back of your closet. You miss him the most on these days and can't help but wonder if he's thinking about you, too. You've been so disciplined since the breakup. You've restrained from calling a few hundred times, and when you have called, you've always hung up before he answered. And though you may have driven past his house, umm... let's say forty-five thousand times to see if his car was there, you never actually stopped. So you deserve to write him a letter or make just one tiny phone call just to say hi and see how he's doing...
NO WAY.

You have worked way too hard to give him the satisfaction that little phone call or "thinking of you" card would provide. It may sound trivial, but a thousand things could go wrong. If you call, your voice could quiver or tears may fall; there's no way of knowing before you dial. If you write, you are essentially giving him back a piece of your heart, a small token that shows you still care. He expects the phone call and the letter, and you must remember this... you do not want to be predictable.

So sit down somewhere quiet with a notebook and a pen and write away. Tell him how you feel, how much he hurt you and how huge a mistake you think he made. Tell him how long it has taken to get yourself together, but that you are almost there. Tell him that you don't need him to love you for you to love yourself. Don't forget to put in how perfect you look in the new jeans you bought with the money you would've spent on his birthday gift. And lastly, thank him for making you happy at one point in your life, but for also showing you, by leaving, how fantastic life can really be... and the most important and hardest part: truly believe each and every word you put down on that paper.

Leave the letter for a few hours — a day even — and then come back to it. Be proud of your words and how far you have come in this long breakup process. Then rip the letter to shreds or set fire to it and watch it fade away. Don't think that by not sending it, he will never know how you feel. He knows... and if he doesn't know right now, he will sometime soon. Your silence, your absence from his life, is proof enough — and that alone should let you breathe a sigh of relief.

Girls' Night Out

You have wallowed in self-pity long enough. You have spent enough time getting to know yourself. You have done enough crunches and eaten enough salads to be on the cover of a trendy fashion magazine. You are ready for a night on the town. A night that will completely take your mind off anything negative. A night where the only thing that matters is fun, fun, fun.

Call all your closest girlfriends early in the week and let them know that you are ready for the night of your life. Pick a night that everyone can attend and tell them you will begin the night at your house. The last time most of them were over at your house, you were knee-deep in tissues, sucking down quarts of rocky road fudge swirl like it was water. You are a different person now, and this is your time to shine.

Pamper yourself the day of your big night. Soak in the tub, paint your nails, and pluck your brows. Dress in your sexiest skirt and top and don't leave the house before looking in the mirror and telling yourself that you look hot this evening. You know you do. When the girls arrive, truly enjoy their company. Don't waste one breath talking about your ex — unless, of course, it is to say how awful he looked the last time you saw him or what an airhead his new Barbie-Doll girlfriend is. Always remember what this night is about... a celebration of single and loving it... well, almost loving it.

This night is not a time to seek out a new mate or to figure out where your ex will be and flirt with all his friends. This night is a "ladies' night" so to speak. This is a night to celebrate how wonderful it is to be a single woman; a free-spirited, joyous, beautiful, single woman. Don't waste any time thinking about... (what's his name again?) In other words, you are no longer a dumpee — you are a survivor, and if at any point in the night you find your mind wandering, ask the DJ to play your song...

I Will Survive

At first I was afraid, I was petrified
Kept thinkin' I could never live without you by my side
But then I spent so many nights thinkin' how you did me wrong
And I grew strong, and I learned how to get along
And so you're back from outer space
I just walked in to find you here with that sad look
    upon your face
I should have changed that stupid lock
I should have made you leave your key
If I'd known for just one second you'd be back to bother me
Go on now, go. Walk out the door.
Just turn around now cause you're not welcome anymore
Weren't you the one who tried to hurt me with goodbye
Did you think I'd crumble?
Did you think I'd lay down and die?
Oh no, not I. I will survive

Oh as long as I know how to love I know I'll stay alive
I've got all my life to live. I've got all my love to give
And I'll survive. I will survive. Hey, hey.
It took all the strength I had not to fall apart
Kept trying hard to mend the pieces of my broken heart
And I spent oh so many nights just feeling sorry for myself
I used to cry, but now I hold my head up high.
And you see me, somebody new,
I'm not that chained up little person still in love with you
And so you felt like dropping in and just expect me to be free
Now I'm saving all my lovin' for someone who's lovin' me

I will survive. I will survive. Hey, hey.

— *Dino Fekaris and Freddie Perren*

Change Is a Chance to Grow

You are free. You must think free. There is no longer someone to check in with before making plans or someone to call when you get home at night. There is no longer the need to save money for some extravagant, very meaningful gift or to spend money on itchy lace undergarments. You are free, and despite the brief pangs of lost love, it is a wonderful thing. It is time to take full advantage and do the things you've always wanted to do, as well as the things you didn't even know you wanted to do.

Read up on local events. You will be surprised at the exciting things going on in your neighborhood. Visit museums and art galleries. There are so many opportunities right in front of your nose — chances to learn new things and meet new people. Look into taking classes at a local college or community recreational center. Explore a hobby you've always enjoyed, such as pottery or photography, or take up a sport like tennis or golf. These are great ways to meet interesting people and cultivate new relationships. After a long day of work or school, it may be hard to find the motivation to do these things, but once you get yourself into a pattern, you will look forward to this time to unwind. If you keep yourself busy, you will only have enough time to think about yourself... not about your ex.

You have the freedom to be utterly spontaneous, impulsive, and downright silly. You can relax when you want to relax, brood when you want to brood, dance when you want to dance. Private moments are the only times in which you are in total control of what you feel, think, and do, and if not, there is nobody else to blame.

— *Jeffrey Kottler, Ph.D.*

Time Passes...
The Heart Heals

The loneliness that sometimes comes
because of love is a more painful thing.
Everything is black, wizened, rutted,
petrified, by-tracked, and ruined: the hours are
cruel, ambiguous, solitary — and the voices
of love hang silent in the crass dark.
But this loneliness is a brief thing.
Where darkness flourishes, the light breaks.
Where the heart lies tufted to wrack, joy is unlocked.
Time pulses and opens like a new bloom —
and everything glows with a richness of feeling.

— Rolando A. Carbonell

Go Fishing

The problem with beginning to date again is not going to be finding a man. Be assured that swimming in those "singles-only" waters are plenty of good-looking, well-educated, well-dressed, interesting fish. The problem is going to be figuring out when you are ready to dive in.

Your days may now consist of being dragged to singles bars by your concerned friends and going on blind dates with the sons of the women in your mother's bingo group. And as appealing as all that may sound, all you can think about is your ex.

News Flash You are not ready to be dating... yet. *Yet* is the key word here.

One broken heart will not brand you single forever, though there is no way of saying exactly how long it will take for you to be able to look into another man's eyes and feel the jitters instead of complete nausea. It takes a bit of experimenting, but the important thing is to be honest with yourself and with those you choose to invite into your life.

At first you will find yourself comparing every man you meet to your ex, and no one will come close to the perfect, God-like image he has become in your head since his departure. You have long forgotten all of the annoying habits and little quirks that once drove you insane. He wasn't perfect then, and he is definitely less than perfect now, so searching for a replacement is not what you want to be doing.

Take your time when getting to know new people. You are fully capable of being alone, and there is no reason to rush into a relationship that will not benefit you and your life. Survey the seas. You have every right to be choosy. Your overall experience with your ex should give you some insight into what you do or do not want in your life. If you see someone who looks like he's worth getting to know, be aggressive and see what he's all about. At this point, you have nothing to lose. Play the field and have fun.

Remember This...

After a while you learn
the subtle difference between
holding a hand and chaining a soul
and you learn
that love doesn't mean leaning
and company doesn't always mean security.
And you begin to learn
that kisses aren't contracts
and presents aren't promises
and you begin to accept your defeats
with your head up and your eyes ahead
with the grace of a woman, not the grief of a child
and you learn
to build all your roads on today
because tomorrow's ground is
too uncertain for plans
and futures have a way of falling down
in mid-flight.

After a while you learn
that even sunshine burns
if you get too much
so you plant your own garden
and decorate your own soul
instead of waiting for someone
to bring you flowers.
And you learn that you really can endure
you really are strong
you really do have worth
and you learn
and you learn
with every goodbye, you learn.

— *Veronica A. Shoffstall*

May the strength
that carried you through this journey
carry you through life...
always.

ACKNOWLEDGMENTS

We gratefully acknowledge the permission granted by the following authors, publishers, and authors' representatives to reprint poems or excerpts from their publications.

Simon & Schuster for "There always comes a time..." and "Yesterday, I Cried" from YESTERDAY, I CRIED by Iyanla Vanzant. Copyright © 1988 by Inner Visions Worldwide Network, Inc. All rights reserved.

Rita Rosencrantz Literary Agency for "The After Math: Breakup Algebra" from HE LOVED ME, HE LOVES ME NOT by Lynn Harris, published by Simon & Schuster, Inc. Copyright © 1996 by Lynn Harris. All rights reserved.

Impact Publishers, Inc., for "Accept... that loneliness..." from REBUILDING: WHEN YOUR RELATIONSHIP ENDS (3rd Edition) by Bruce Fisher. Copyright © 1999 by Bruce Fisher, Ed.D., and Robert E. Alberti, Ph.D. All rights reserved.

Barbara Hansen, Ph.D. for "Even though unwanted loss..." from PICKING UP THE PIECES: HEALING OURSELVES AFTER PERSONAL LOSS, published by Taylor Publishing Company. Copyright © 1990 by Barbara Hansen, Ph.D. All rights reserved.

Chronicle Books, LLC, San Francisco, for "Things to Do with..." and "Date Yourself with Style and Sensitivity" from BAD GIRL'S GUIDE TO GETTING WHAT YOU WANT by Cameron Tuttle. Copyright © 2000 by Cameron Tuttle. All rights reserved.

Crown Publishers, a division of Random House, Inc., for "Focus on those things..." from 365 WAYS TO CHANGE YOUR LIFE by Suzanne Somers. Copyright © 1999 by Suzanne Somers. All rights reserved. And for "One Will Pass the Door" from THE DESIDERATA OF HOPE by Max Ehrmann. Copyright 1948 by Bertha K. Ehrmann. Copyright © renewed 1976 by Robert L. Bell. All rights reserved.

Celestial Arts for "Whoever we are..." from FAREWELLS ARE ONLY BEGINNINGS by George Betts. Copyright © 1976 by George Betts. All rights reserved.

HarperCollins Publishers, Inc., and Abner Stein for "Do All the Things He Always Hated" from GETTING OVER JOHN DOE by Suzanne Yalof. Copyright © 1999 by Suzanne Yalof. All rights reserved.

Universal Music Publishing Group, Inc., for "I Will Survive." Words and Music by Frederick J. Perren and Dino Fekaris. Copyright © 1978 by Universal-Polygram International Publishing, Inc. on behalf of Itself and Perren-Vibes Music, Inc. (ASCAP) International copyright secured. All rights reserved.

Jeremy P. Tarcher, a division of Penguin Putnam, Inc., for "You have the freedom..." from PRIVATE MOMENTS, SECRET SELVES by Jeffrey Kottler. Copyright © 1990 by Jeffrey Kottler. All rights reserved.

Creative Development Institute of the Philippines for "The loneliness that sometimes..." from BEYOND FORGETTING by Rolando A. Carbonell. Copyright © 1961 by Rolando A. Carbonell. All rights reserved.

Veronica A. Shoffstall for "After a while..." Copyright © 1971 by Veronica A. Shoffstall. All rights reserved.

A careful effort has been made to trace the ownership of selections used in this anthology in order to obtain permission to reprint copyrighted material and give proper credit to the copyright owners. If any error or omission has occurred, it is completely inadvertent, and we would like to make corrections in future editions provided that written notification is made to the publisher:

SPS STUDIOS, INC., P.O. Box 4549, Boulder, Colorado 80306.